Christmas
Praise

Christmas Praise

Worship Resources for the
Seasons of Christmas

Edited by
WALDO BEACH

WESTMINSTER/JOHN KNOX PRESS   LOUISVILLE, KENTUCKY

Book design by Publishers' WorkGroup

First edition

Published by Westminster/John Knox Press
Louisville, Kentucky

PRINTED IN THE UNITED STATES OF AMERICA

9 8 7 6 5 4 3 2 1

Library of Congress Cataloging-in-Publication Data

Christmas praise : worship resources for the seasons of Christmas / edited by Waldo Beach. — 1st ed.
    p.   cm.
  Includes indexes.
  ISBN 0-664-21939-X

  1. Christmas. 2. Advent. 3. Epiphany season. I. Beach, Waldo.
BV40.C48 1991
242'.33—dc20   91-6583

Acknowledgments

"A Carol for Children," from *Verses from 1929 On,* by Ogden Nash, copyright © 1934 by Ogden Nash. First published in *The New Yorker.* Reprinted by permission of Little, Brown and Company.

"A Cycle of Praise," from *Holy Merriment,* by Arnold Kenseth. © 1963 University of North Carolina Press. Reprinted by permission.

"Christmas Prayer," by Bishop Ralph Spaulding Cushman, reprinted by permission of Robert E. Cushman.

"The Flight Into Egypt," from "For the Time Being: A Christmas Oratorio," in *W. H. Auden: Collected Poems,* edited by Edward Mendelson. Copyright © 1976 by Edward Mendelson, William Meredith and Monroe K. Spears, executors of the Estate of W. H. Auden. Reprinted by permission of Random House, Inc., New York, and Faber and Faber Ltd., London.

"Noel: Christmas Eve, 1913," from *October and Other Poems,* by Robert Bridges, London: William Heinemann Ltd., 1920. Reprinted by permission of the publisher.

"O Simplicitas," from *The Weather of the Heart,* by Madeleine L'Engle, © 1978 by Crosswicks. Used by permission of Harold Shaw Publishers, Wheaton, Illinois.

"Only an Hour," from "Two Christmas Carols," copyright 1941 Robinson Jeffers. From *Be Angry at the Sun, and Other Poems,* published by Random House. Reprinted by permission of Jeffers Literary Properties.

"Soliloquy" and "Visit of the Shepherds," by Marian Darling, reprinted by permission of the author.

"The Christmas Star," by Nancy Byrd Turner. Used by permission of the author.

Contents

Christmas

Epiphany

Preface

This anthology of worship resources is intended for use in churches and homes to celebrate Christmas in a manner more authentic than is the current prevailing practice. In America today the honoring of the Incarnation has been profaned by commercialism. Advent is a time when we are flooded and harassed by alluring reminders that only so many shopping days are left till Christmas. The heart is turned to the shopping mall rather than to the manger of Bethlehem. To most children, Santa Claus and Rudolph the red-nosed reindeer may be figures more familiar than Joseph, Mary, and the baby Jesus. Few know what Epiphany means. Yet Christmastide is a very holy time of the Christian year. It should not be desecrated but be observed in holy merriment. For this reason one must turn away from the crass and the gaudy to Holy Scripture, to the great lyric expressions of Christmas praise found in verse, in hymns and carols, in prayer and litany.

The three main segments of this anthology follow the sequence of the traditional Christian year calendar: Advent, Christmas, and Epiphany. The Advent materials are suited for the weeks prior to Christmas Day. The Christmas materials are best used for a Christmas Eve service and for the twelve days from December 25 to January 5, which may include one or two Sundays after Christmas, depending on how the calendar dates fall out. Epiphany is a day, January 6, that brings to an end the Christmas cycle. The word "Epiphany" means, of course, the "showing forth" or "manifestation" of God's spirit in Christ. It is a day to recall the visit of the three Magi to Bethlehem and Christ's being made known to all people. The Sundays immediately following Epiphany, while they do not properly constitute a season, have traditionally been used—through the lectionary readings—to reflect on the beginnings of Jesus' ministry: recalling the baptism of Christ by John in the River Jordan, and the first recorded miracle, his turning the water into wine at the wedding in Cana.

The materials for each of the sections are in the following sequence:

1. Selected scripture references from the standard lectionary readings, which are now more and more in common church use, come first. Not all of the "official" prescribed lectionary readings for each Sunday are given, only those that are the source and inspiration of the poetry, hymns, carols, litanies, and prayers that follow.

2. A group of poems follows, some old and some contemporary, that cast into lyric form the rich nuances of meaning inspired by the Incarnation. There is a vast treasury of Christmas poems on which one might draw. These few are chosen to illustrate the wide variety of meanings and insights with which poets have honored the holy season.

3. Next is a selection of hymns and carols. Again, from the vast reservoir of Christmas music found in hymnals and carols collections, the editor has chosen only a few. Some are familiar ones that can be readily sung by the congregation or by a family gathering, although the most familiar old favorites are not included. Others are new, a few composed by the editor, setting into song some texts of modern poets. Some may be more suitable for the church choir to sing as part of the worship service.

This anthology of resources is intended for use in Christian churches of all denominations. Many of the familiar hymns and carols in this anthology are to be found in the standard hymnals of the Protestant churches: *The Lutheran Book of Worship* (1978); *The United Methodist Hymnal* (1989); *the Presbyterian Hymnal* (Presbyterian (U.S.A.), 1990); *the Hymnal 1982* (Protestant Episcopal, 1985); *The Broadman Hymnal* (Baptist, 1975); and *The Hymnal of the United Church of Christ* (1974).

Note that there are some variations and revisions of the translations of texts from one hymnal to another. For example, Gracia Grindal's translation of "Lo, How a Rose" has more lyric style than the version usually sung. To enlarge the circle of the familiar, the editor has included several original carols and hymns. To sing a new text to a new and strange tune does not come easily. To teach the congregation a new carol, a trained church musician may well set a new text to a familiar tune, making sure that the meter of the text fits the meter of the tune. Or the choir may sing the new text with the new tune as a way of acquainting the congregation with new songs. Also, when the leader of worship reads aloud the text of the old or new hymn or carol before it is sung, the import of its meaning in the singing is greatly enriched.

4. Finally, a group of prayers and antiphonal litanies concludes each section. Most of the prayers are in the collect form. These worship resources can be used by the leader of worship in whatever arrangement seems most appropriate. Some of them may be included as part of the

larger, more conventional structures of the service of worship, including the sermon.

There are also certain liturgical practices rich in meaning that may be observed, such as the lighting of the four Advent candles in sequence during the four Sundays of Advent. Many of the items in this anthology are suitable for a Christmas Eve candlelight service that might be based on the Johannine text (John 1:1–14) concerning God's light coming into the world. Such a service could commence with the sanctuary darkened and only a single candle burning, from which other candles are lit by the spreading of lights out to the altar, to window candelabras, and finally, at the close of the service, to the individual candles in the hands of all present. The gradual spreading and sharing of God's light in the world of darkness through the birth of Christ is thereby symbolized. For the musical part of the worship, instruments such as the recorder, flute, and harp can provide descants or obbligatos to the organ or piano accompanying choir or congregational singing.

The celebration of the seasons of Christmas need not be limited to church services. It is hoped that the materials in this volume will be of value in celebrating Christmas at home, in the family circle or with a group of neighbors. For many years it has been a joyous custom during Advent in this editor's own household to have a Christmas sing, where reasonably talented friends gather to sing, in four-part harmony, both familiar and unfamiliar carols (a few of which are contained in this volume), and where some poems are read.

Homes can become sanctuaries for worship as much as churches. A family might gather around a Christmas tree either on Christmas Eve or on Christmas morning. Susan might read a poem or one of the lectionary texts and John read another, Dad lead in prayer, and the family sing one or two familiar carols. This would be a more authentic act of Christmas praise and shared joy than the usual early-morning rush of the children to find what Santa stuffed in the stocking by the fireplace. In the ways we have suggested to counter the usual spoilage of Christmas by materialism, the hearths of our homes can become altars and the blessed season may be honored in holy tribute to the birth of Christ.

Advent

ADVENT LECTIONARY READINGS

Old Testament

Isaiah 11:1–10; 40:1–11; 61:1–3, 10–11
Jeremiah 33:14–16
Malachi 3:1–4

New Testament

Luke 1:46–55; 1:67–79

A Cycle of Praise

The roads of our village amble
Through views of four seasons.
The eye loves and follows
The ritual year through occasions
That dazzle all seeing, humble
All knowing. Changes are heard:
Spring drums in the little hollows,
The to-and-fro borne bird
Of summer chirrs, the pageant
Autumn trumpets on the hill.
All sceneries lie urgent
On the heart. All are a praise
To Him whose laughter wills
Our glory-be of days.

Especially now do we feel
His sounding joy and His dare:
When sun-dials point winter
And daylights grow fainter;
When Advent hallows our streets
In a snowfall of prayers.
From windows our fir trees
Wink azure devotions,
Because His birth bells peal
Alarums of love at our gates,
And we wake with His innocence
In us. The year ends here,
But we begin, in the air's dance
Of bright adorations.

Arnold Kenseth

The Song of Mary
Luke 1:46–55

In joy my soul gives praises to the Lord.
My heart will sing in hallowing his name.
His grace has chosen me as holy ward,
And one of humble mien shall have the fame
Of honored memory. From heaven's height,
As sign and signal of his loving will,
He favors me, the one to bear the light
For those who waited long and trust him still.

The proud and mighty kings he has dethroned;
The humble and the plain he lifts on high.
Of his abundance he sustains the poor
And seizes from the wealthy all they owned.
So shall his word, in ages past and nigh,
Be kept and blest as long as days endure.

Waldo Beach

Soliloquy

Stubborn of me to insist on Christmas,
When I can only stumble through a
  carol-cluttered store
By stopping my ears,
And green plastic garlands twist me into knots.
Love can't be wrapped;
Hate shouldn't be gilded.
The lonely have a right
To leave their dribs and drabs of memories asleep.
But tonight I walked where blowing ebony oaks
Crisscrossed the cold pink sky.
An early Christmas tree
Suddenly pricked the dusk with stars.
I've hurried home to light my candle.

Marian Darling

Advent Sonnet

On coming to Christmas, misled, we forget
That the birth of God's son was not lovely at all.
A stench filled the gloom of the bleak manger stall.
There was blood on the straw and a halo of sweat
Around Mary's head. Soon, warned they should flee
To escape Herod's sword, by stealth in the night
The family of God was driven to flight,
As from Bethlehem's inn outcast, refugee.

But as birth of new life is sprung out of pain,
And faith out of fear, so now, once again,
If we come to the stable by way of the cross
And dismantle our spirits of tinsel and dross,
We can join with glad hearts and exuberant voice
To sing with the heavenly choir, "Rejoice!"

Waldo Beach

Our Lady

Mother of God! no lady thou:
    Common woman of common earth!
"Our Lady" ladies call thee now,
    But Christ was never of gentle birth;
    A common man of the common earth.

For God's ways are not as our ways.
    The noblest lady in the land
Would have given up half her days,
    Would have cut off her right hand,
    To bear the Child that was God of the land.

Never a lady did He choose,
    Only a maid of low degree,
So humble she might not refuse
    The carpenter of Galilee.
    A daughter of the people, she.

Out she sang the song of her heart.
    Never a lady so had sung.
She knew no letters, had no art;
    To all mankind, in woman's tongue,
    Hath Israelitish Mary sung.

And still for men to come she sings,
    Nor shall her singing pass away.
"He hath filled the hungry with good things"—
    Oh, listen, lords and ladies gay!—
    "And the rich He hath sent empty away."

Mary Elizabeth Coleridge

Noel: Christmas Eve, 1913

A frosty Christmas Eve
  when the stars were shining
Fared I forth alone
  where westward falls the hill,
And from many a village
  in the water'd valley
Distant music reach'd me,
  peals of bells aringing:
The constellated sounds
  ran sprinkling on earth's floor
As the dark vault above
  with stars was spangled o'er.

Then sped my thought to keep
  that first Christmas of all
When the shepherds watching
  by their folds ere the dawn
Heard music in the fields
  and marveling could not tell
Whether it were angels
  or the bright stars singing.

Now blessed be the tow'rs
  that crown England so fair,
That stand up strong in prayer
  unto God for our souls:
Blessed be their founders
  (said I) an' our country folk
Who are ringing for Christ
  in the belfries to-night
With arms lifted to clutch
  the rattling ropes that race
Into the dark above
  and the mad romping din.

But to me heard afar
    it was starry music,
Angels' song, comforting
    as the comfort of Christ
When he spake tenderly
    to his sorrowful flock:
The old words came to me
    by the riches of time
Mellow'd and transfigured
    as I stood on the hill
Heark'ning in the aspect
    of th' eternal silence.

Robert Bridges

O Come, O Come, Emmanuel

VENI EMMANUEL   LM with refrain

Latin, c. 12th century
Stanzas 1–2 trans. John Mason Neale, 1851; alt. 1854
Stanza 3 trans. Henry Sloane Coffin, 1916

15th century French
Arr. and harm. Thomas Helmore, 1854

1. O come, O come, Em - man - u - el, And ran-som cap-tive
2. O come, thou Day-spring, come and cheer Our spir - its by thine
3. O come, De - sire of na - tions, bind All peo-ples in one

Is - ra - el, That mourns in lone - ly ex - ile here
ad - vent here; Dis - perse the gloom - y clouds of night,
heart and mind; Bid en - vy, strife, and dis - cord cease;

Refrain

Un - til the Son of God ap - pear.
And death's dark shad - ows put to flight. Re - joice! Re - joice! Em -
Fill the whole world with heav - en's peace.

man - u - el Shall come to thee, O Is - ra - el.

Savior of the Nations, Come

NUN KOMM, DER HEIDEN HEILAND   7.7.7.7

Stanzas 1, 2 Martin Luther, 1523
Trans. William Reynolds, 1851
Stanzas 3–5 Martin L. Seltz, 1969

Enchiridion Oder Handbüchlein, 1524
Harm. J. S. Bach; alt.

1. Sav - ior of the na - tions, come; Vir - gin's Son, here make thy home! Mar - vel now, O heaven and earth, That the Lord chose such a birth.

2. Not by hu - man flesh and blood; By the Spir - it of our God Was the Word of God made flesh, Wom-an's off - spring, pure and fresh.

3. Won - drous birth! O won - drous Child Of the Vir - gin un - de - filed! Hu - man and di - vine in one, Ea - ger now his race to run!

4. God the Fa - ther is his source, Back to God he runs his course; Down to death and hell de - scends, God's high throne he re - as - cends.

5. Now thy man - ger's ha - lo bright Hal - lows night with new - born light; Let no night this light sub - due, Let our faith shine ev - er new.

Text: Stanzas 3–5 © 1969 Concordia Publishing House. Reprinted by permission.

25

Wake, Awake, for Night Is Flying

WACHET AUF   Irregular

Philipp Nicolai, 1599
Trans. by Catherine Winkworth, 1858

Attr. Philipp Nicolai, 1599
Harm. J. S. Bach, 1731

1. Wake, a-wake, for night is fly-ing; The watch-men on the heights are cry-ing: A-wake, Je-ru-sa-lem, at last! Mid-night hears the wel-come voic-es And at the thrill-ing cry re-joic-es; Come forth, ye vir-gins, night is past;

2. Zi-on hears the watch-men sing-ing, And all her heart with joy is spring-ing; She wakes, she ris-es from her gloom; For her Lord comes down all-glo-rious, The strong in grace, in truth vic-to-rious. Her Star is risen; her Light is come.

3. Now let all the heavens a-dore thee, And saints and an-gels sing be-fore thee, With harp and cym-bal's clear-est tone; Of one pearl each shin-ing por-tal, Where we are with the choir im-mor-tal Of an-gels round thy daz-zling throne;

The Bride - groom comes, a - wake; Your lamps with glad - ness take:
Ah come, thou bless - ed One, God's own be - lov - ed Son:
Nor eye hath seen, nor ear Hath yet at - tained to hear

Al - le - lu - ia! And for his mar - riage feast pre - pare,
Al - le - lu - ia! We fol - low till the halls we see
What there is ours; But we re - joice and sing to thee

For ye must go and meet him there.
Where thou hast bid us sup with thee.
Our hymn of joy e - ter - nal - ly.

27

Come, Thou Long-Expected Jesus

HYFRYDOL   8.7.8.7 D

Charles Wesley, 1744

Rowland Hugh Pritchard, 1831

1. Come, Thou long - ex - pect - ed Je - sus, Born to set Thy
2. Born Thy peo - ple to de - liv - er, Born a child and

peo - ple free; From our fears and sins re - lease us;
yet a King, Born to reign in us for - ev - er,

Let us find our rest in Thee. Is - rael's strength and con - so -
Now Thy gra - cious king - dom bring. By Thine own e - ter - nal

la - tion, Hope of all the earth Thou art; Dear de - sire of
Spir - it Rule in all our hearts a - lone; By Thine all - suf -

ev - ery na - tion, Joy of ev - ery long - ing heart.
fi - cient mer - it Raise us to Thy glo - rious throne.

On Jordan's Bank the Baptist's Cry

PUER NOBIS NASCITUR   LM

Charles Coffin, 1676–1749
Trans. composite

Trier ms., 15th century
Adapt. Michael Praetorius, 1609
Harm. George Ratcliffe Woodward, 1910

1. On Jordan's bank the Baptist's cry Announces that the Lord is nigh; A-wake and heark-en, for he brings Glad tid-ings of the King of kings!

2. Then cleansed be ev-ery life from sin; Make straight the way for God with-in, And let us all our hearts pre-pare For Christ to come and en-ter there.

3. We hail you as our Sav-ior, Lord, Our ref-uge, and our great re-ward; O let your face up-on us shine And fill the world with love di-vine.

4. All praise to you e-ter-nal Son, Whose ad-vent has our free-dom won, Whom with the Fa-ther we a-dore, And Ho-ly Spir-it, ev-er-more.

The Angel Gabriel from Heaven Came

GABRIEL'S MESSAGE   10.10.12.10

Basque Noel

Sabine Baring-Gould (1834–1924)

Arr. C. E. Pettman (1866–1943)

1. The an - gel Ga - bri - el from heav - en came, His
2. "Fear not, for you shall bear a ho - ly child, By
3. Then gen - tle Ma - ry hum - bly bowed her head: "To
4. "And so," she said, "how hap - py I shall be! All
5. Of her, Em-man - u - el, the Christ, was born In

wings as drift - ed snow, his eyes as flame:
him shall man to God be rec - on - ciled,
me be as it pleas - es God," she said,
gen - er - a - tions will re - mem - ber me,
Beth - le - hem, up - on that Christ - mas morn.

"From God, all hail," the an - gel said to Ma - ry, "Most
His name shall be Em - man - u - el, the long fore - told: Most
"My soul shall praise and mag - ni - fy his ho - ly name." Most
For God has kept the prom - is - es to Is - ra - el." Most
And Chris-tian folk through-out the world will ev - er say, "Most

high - ly fa - vored la - dy!" Glo - ri - a!
high - ly fa - vored la - dy!" Glo - ri - a!
high - ly fa - vored la - dy! Glo - ri - a!
high - ly fa - vored la - dy! Glo - ri - a!
high - ly fa - vored la - dy!" Glo - ri - a!

Lift Up Your Heads, Ye Mighty Gates

TRURO   LM

Georg Weissel, 1642
Trans. Catherine Winkworth, 1855; alt.

Psalmodia Evangelica, 1789
Thomas Williams, 1789
Harm. Lowell Mason (1792–1872)

1. Lift up your heads, ye might - y gates, Be - hold, the
2. O blest the land, the cit - y blest, Where Christ the
3. Fling wide the por - tals of your heart; Make it a
4. Re - deem - er, come! I o - pen wide My heart to

King of glo - ry waits; The King of kings is
rul - er is con - fessed! O hap - py hearts and
tem - ple, set a - part From earth - ly use for
thee; here, Lord, a - bide. Let me thy in - ner

draw - ing near; The Sav - ior of the world is here!
hap - py homes To whom this King in tri - umph comes.
heaven's em - ploy, A - dorned with prayer, and love, and joy.
pres - ence feel; thy grace and love in me re - veal.

Magnificat Now

TUGWOOD LM

Fred Kaan

Nicholas Gatty

1. Sing we a song of high re - volt; Make great the
2. Sing we of him who deep - ly cares And still with
3. By him the poor are lift - ed up; He sat - is -
4. He calls us to re - volt and fight With him for

Lord, his name ex - alt! Sing we the song that Ma - ry
us our bur - den bears. He who with strength the proud dis -
fies with bread and cup The hun - gry folk of man - y
what is just and right, To sing and live Mag - ni - fi -

sang Of God at war with hu - man wrong.
owns, Brings down the might - y from their thrones.
lands; The rich must go with emp - ty hands.
cat In crowd - ed street and dis - mal flat.

Tell Out, My Soul

WOODLANDS 10.10.10.10

Timothy Dudley-Smith, 1969

Walter Greatorex, 1916

no

1. Tell out, my soul, the great-ness of the Lord: Un - num - bered
2. Tell out, my soul, the great-ness of his name: Make known his
3. Tell out, my soul, the great-ness of his might: Powers and do -
4. Tell out, my soul, the great-ness of his word: Firm is his

bless - ings give my spir - it voice; Ten - der to me the
might, the deeds his arm hath done; His mer - cy sure, from
min - ions lay their glo - ry by; Proud hearts and stub - born
prom - ise, and his mer - cy sure. Tell out, my soul, the

prom - ise of his word; In God my Sav - ior shall my heart re - joice.
age to age the same; His ho - ly name, the Lord, the might - y one.
wills are put to flight, The hun - gry fed, the hum - ble lift - ed high.
great - ness of the Lord To chil - dren's chil - dren and for - ev - er - more.

Advent Prayers

Almighty God, who through the prophets spoke the promise of a
Messiah to come to free your people from bondage, stir us through their
words, we pray, to prepare our hearts in eager waiting, that our hopes
may be sustained through the dark days of winter by their assurance of
the bright day of the coming of our Lord, in whose name we pray.
Amen.

In this holy season of Advent, O God, clear our spirits from the
concerns over material things, the trinkets and the tinsel, all that hide
from our sight the vision of your Word made flesh, so that like the
shepherds we may travel light to Bethlehem, bringing only the pure and
simple devotions of faith and hope and love. *Amen.*

Almighty God, author of peace and lover of concord, who through the
voices of the prophets foretold the coming of one who would speak
peace to the nations, turn our hearts from pride of national power, from
the madness of war, from a foolish trust in the security of arms, that we
may be ready to celebrate his birth when he comes, the Prince of Peace,
even Jesus Christ our Lord. *Amen.*

Creator God, whose spirit in the blessed Mary evoked her song of
praise, that she should bear the Savior of your people, enable us to join
her in glad celebration of joy and anticipation, that we, like her in
humility and devotion, may also be bearers of your word and spirit
incarnate in our lives. *Amen.*

A Litany for Advent

LEADER: As we come to the glorious seasons of Christmas, O Lord, we ask your forgiveness for all the trivial concerns that clutter our minds and hearts, and so deafen our ears that we fail to hear the prophet's words of promise of a Messiah to come who can redeem our lives.

PEOPLE: Have mercy on us, O God.

LEADER: For our narrow vision of neighborhood, where we seek to serve only ourselves in comfort, and fail to heed the cries of the poor and the hungry and the homeless, and thus are ill prepared to receive the one who comes to proclaim liberty to those captive to poverty, who will usher in the kingdom of righteousness and equity, and who will reveal the glory of the Lord to all humankind,

PEOPLE: Have mercy on us, O God.

LEADER: Teach us, in this Advent season, to find beauty in simplicity, to find riches in plain living, to find self-worth in self-giving, that we may be truly prepared for the day of our Lord's coming, who came not as a mighty king but as a child born in a cowshed, and who gave his life as servant for our salvation.

PEOPLE: Grant this, we pray, in his name, Amen.

A Litany of Confession for Advent

LEADER: Let us join in a common confession of our sins. For the arrogance of our pride of race, of nation, and of class, by which we put down others not of our kind and thus break the community of the human family, in defiance of your will,

PEOPLE: Lord, forgive us.

LEADER: For the sin of our self-concern, where we seek first our own private good, in getting and gaining, to the neglect of our neighbor's needs near and far,

PEOPLE: Lord, forgive us.

LEADER: For the sin of our cruel deceit and bland hypocrisy, where we speak of making peace while building weapons of war and mass destruction,

PEOPLE: Lord, forgive us.

LEADER: For our lust for the comforts of the flesh that both starve our spirits in the glut of things and neglect the hungry and the poor,

PEOPLE: Lord, forgive us.

LEADER: For our casual and careless disdain for the good earth, in all its majesty and beauty, which we plunder and despoil for present gain, counting not the dire cost the future must pay,

PEOPLE: Lord, forgive us.

ALL: As we come again to this blessed season celebrating the birth of Christ, cleanse us, we pray, from these and all our other sins, that we may be prepared in our hearts to welcome his coming in spirit and in truth, and to turn from our evil ways to new ways of life, obedient to your holy will made known in Christ, in whose name we pray. Amen.

Christmas

CHRISTMAS LECTIONARY READINGS

Old Testament

Psalms 96, 97, 98, 111

New Testament

Matthew 1:18–23
Luke 2:1–20
John 1:1–14

O Simplicitas

An angel came to me
And I was unprepared
To be what God was using.
Mother I was to be.
A moment I despaired,
Thought briefly of refusing.
The angel knew I heard.
According to God's Word
I bowed to this strange choosing.

A palace should have been
The birthplace of a king
(I had no way of knowing).
We went to Bethlehem;
It was so strange a thing.
The wind was cold, and blowing,
My cloak was old, and thin.
They turned us from the inn;
The town was overflowing.

God's Word, a child so small,
Who still must learn to speak,
Lay in humiliation.
Joseph stood, strong and tall.
The beasts were warm and meek
And moved with hesitation.
The Child born in a stall?
I understood it all.
Kings came in adoration.

Perhaps it was absurd:
The stable set apart,
The sleepy cattle lowing;
And the incarnate Word
Resting against my heart.
My joy was overflowing.
The shepherds came, adored
The folly of the Lord,
Wiser than all men's knowing.

Madeleine L'Engle

The Christmas Story

Tell again the Christmas story:
Christ is born in all His glory!
Baby laid in Manger dark,
Lighting centuries with the spark
Of innocence that is the Child
Trusting all within His smile.

Tell again the Christmas story
With the halo of His glory:
Halo born of humbleness
By the breath of cattle blest,
By the poverty of stall
Where a bed of straw is all,
By a door closed at the inn
Where only men of means get in,
By a door closed to the poor
Christ is born on earthen floor
In a stable with no lock—
Yet kingdoms tremble at the shock
Of infant King in swaddling clothes
At an address no one knows
Because there is no painted sign—
Nothing but a star divine,
Nothing but a halo bright
About His young head in the night,
Nothing but the wondrous light
Of innocence that is the Child
Trusting all within His smile.

Mary's Son of golden star:
Wise Men journey from afar!

Mary's Son in Manger born:
Music of an Angel's horn!

Mary's Son in straw and glory:
Wonder of the Christmas story!

Langston Hughes

Visit of the Shepherds

Shyly they tiptoed in,
fathers, to see a child
awkward before this mother
until she smiled.

Then their eyes lighted
and one leaned down to twist
a brittle strand of hay
from the Baby's fist.

Birth-wonder held them,
they did not misconstrue
the glory for the poverty
that Mary knew.

These were the wise men
for they saw
nothing to pity
in the bed of straw.

Marian Darling

Christmas Symbol

Yearlong, the subterranean stream
Flowed silently and hidden,
But now, as wakers from a dream,
We see that Love, unbidden,
Has flooded our dry hearts again,
With grace past all petition.
If God so loved unworthy men,
Hearts must give back contrition,
Accepting Love for Love's sake given,
Else earth has mocked the hopes of heaven.

Elinor Lennen

Only an Hour

For an hour on Christmas Eve
And again on the holy day
Seek the magic of past time,
From this present turn away.
Dark though our day,
Light is the snow on the hawthorn bush
And the ox knelt down at midnight.

Only an hour, only an hour
From wars and confusions turn away
To the islands of old time
When the world was simple and gay,
Or so we say,
And light lay the snow on the green holly,
And tall oxen knelt at midnight.

Caesar and Herod shared the world,
Sorrow over Bethlehem lay,
Iron the empire, brutal the time,
Dark was that day,
Light lay the snow on the mistletoe berries
And the ox knelt down at midnight.

Robinson Jeffers

Christmas Prayer

Let not our hearts be busy inns,
  That have no room for Thee,
But cradles for the living Christ
  And His nativity.

Still driven by a thousand cares
  The pilgrims come and go;
The hurried caravans press on;
  The inns are crowded so!

Here are the rich and busy ones,
  With things that must be sold,
No room for simple things within
  This hostelry of gold.

Yet hunger dwells within these walls,
  These shining walls and bright,
And blindness groping here and there
  Without a ray of light.

Oh, lest we starve, and lest we die,
  In our stupidity,
Come, Holy Child, within and share
  Our hospitality.

Let not our hearts be busy inns,
  That have no room for Thee,
But cradles for the living Christ
  And His nativity.

Ralph Spaulding Cushman

A Carol for Children

God rest you, merry Innocents,
Let nothing you dismay,
Let nothing wound an eager heart
Upon this Christmas day.

Yours be the genial holly wreaths,
The stockings and the tree;
An aged world to you bequeaths
Its own forgotten glee.

Soon, soon enough come crueler gifts,
The anger and the tears;
Between you now there sparsely drifts
A handful yet of years.

Oh, dimly, dimly glows the star
Through the electric throng;
The bidding in temple and bazaar
Drowns out the silver song.

The ancient altars smoke afresh,
The ancient idols stir;
Faint in the reek of burning flesh
Sink frankincense and myrrh.

Gaspar, Balthazar, Melchior!
Where are your offerings now?
What greetings to the Prince of War,
His darkly branded brow?

Two ultimate laws alone we know,
The ledger and the sword—
So far away, so long ago,
We lost the infant Lord.

Only the children clasp His hand;
His voice speaks low to them,
And still for them the shining band
Wings over Bethlehem.

God rest you, merry Innocents,
While innocence endures.
A sweeter Christmas than we to ours
May you bequeath to yours.

Ogden Nash

Christmas Bells

I heard the bells on Christmas Day
Their old, familiar carols play,
   And wild and sweet
   The words repeat
Of peace on earth, good-will to men!

And thought how, as the day had come,
The belfries of all Christendom
   Had rolled along
   The unbroken song,
Of peace on earth, good-will to men!

Till, ringing, singing on its way,
The world revolved from night to day,
   A voice, a chime,
   A chant sublime
Of peace on earth, good-will to men!

Then pealed the bells more loud and deep:
"God is not dead; nor doth he sleep!
   The Wrong shall fail,
   The Right prevail,
With peace on earth, good-will to men!"

Henry Wadsworth Longfellow

The Risk of Birth

Madeleine L'Engle, 1978

Waldo Beach, 1987

1. This is no time for a child to be born,
2. That was no time for a child to be born,
3. When is the time for love to be born?

With the earth be - trayed by war and hate
In a land in the crush - ing grip of Rome;
The inn is full on the plan - et earth,

And a com - et slash - ing the sky to warn
When hon - or and truth were tram - pled to scorn,
And by a com - et the sky is torn—

That time runs out and the sun burns late.
Yet here did the Sav - ior make his home.
Yet Love still takes the risk of birth.

Of the Father's Love Begotten

DIVINUM MYSTERIUM   8.7.8.7.8.7.7

Marcus Aurelius Clemens Prudentius (348–413)
Trans. composite

Plainsong, Mode V, 13th century

1. Of the Fa - ther's love be - got - ten Ere the worlds be -
2. O that birth for - ev - er bless - ed, When the Vir - gin,
3. This is he whom seers in old time Chant-ed of with
4. Let the heights of heaven a - dore him; An - gel hosts, his
5. Christ, to thee, with God the Fa - ther, And, O Ho - ly

gan to be, He is Al - pha and O - me - ga,
full of grace, By the Ho - ly Ghost con - ceiv - ing,
one ac - cord, Whom the voic - es of the proph - ets
prais - es sing; Powers, do - min - ions, bow be - fore him
Ghost, to thee, Hymn and chant and high thanks-giv - ing

He the source, the end - ing he, Of the things that are, that
Bore the Sav - ior of our race, And the Babe, the world's Re -
Prom-ised in their faith - ful word; Now he shines, the long - ex -
And ex - tol our God and King; Let no tongue on earth be
And un - wea - ried prais - es be: Hon - or, glo - ry, and do -

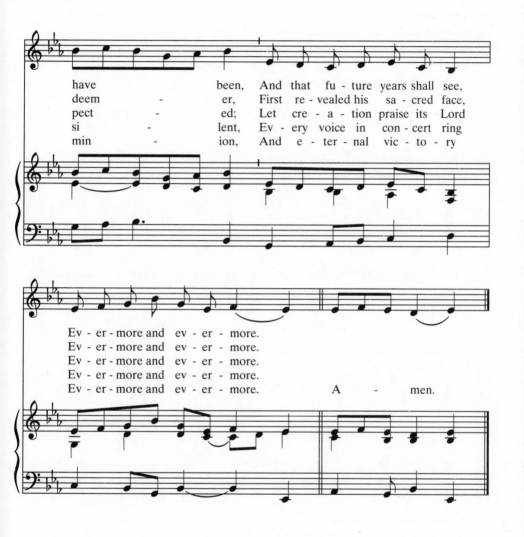

have been, And that fu - ture years shall see,
deem - er, First re - vealed his sa - cred face,
pect - ed; Let cre - a - tion praise its Lord
si - lent, Ev - ery voice in con - cert ring
min - ion, And e - ter - nal vic - to - ry

Ev - er - more and ev - er - more.
Ev - er - more and ev - er - more.
Ev - er - more and ev - er - more.
Ev - er - more and ev - er - more.
Ev - er - more and ev - er - more. A - men.

Lo, How a Rose Is Growing

ES IST EIN' ROS'   7.6.7.6.6.7.6

German, 15th century
Trans. Gracia Grindal, b. 1943

Alte Catholische Geistliche Kirchengesäng
Cologne, 1599

1. Lo, how a rose is grow-ing, A bloom of fin-est grace; The proph-ets had fore-told it: A branch of Jes-se's race Would bear one per-fect flower Here in the cold of win-ter And dark-est mid-night hour.

2. The rose of which I'm sing-ing, I-sa-iah had fore-told. He came to us through Ma-ry Who shel-tered him from cold. Through God's e-ter-nal will This child to us was giv-en At mid-night calm and still.

3. The shep-herds heard the sto-ry The an-gels sang that night: How Christ was born of Ma-ry; He was the Son of light. To Beth-le-hem they ran To find him in the man-ger As an-gel her-alds sang.

4. This flower, so small and ten-der, With fra-grance fills the air; His bright-ness ends the dark-ness That kept the earth in fear. True God and yet true man, He came to save his peo-ple From earth's dark night of sin.

5. O Sav-ior, child of Ma-ry, Who felt all hu-man woe; O Sav-ior, King of glo-ry, Who tri-umphed o'er our foe: Bring us at length, we pray, To the bright courts of heav-en And in-to end-less day.

Once in Royal David's City

IRBY   8.7.8.7.7.7

Cecil Frances Alexander, 1848   Henry John Gauntlett, 1849

1. Once in roy-al Da-vid's cit-y Stood a low-ly cat-tle shed, Where a moth-er laid her ba-by In a man-ger for his bed: Ma-ry was that moth-er mild, Je-sus Christ her lit-tle child.

2. He came down to earth from heav-en Who is God and Lord of all, And his shel-ter was a sta-ble, And his cra-dle was a stall: With the poor and mean and low-ly Lived on earth our Sav-ior ho-ly.

3. And our eyes at last shall see him, Through his own re-deem-ing love; For that child so dear and gen-tle Is our Lord in heaven a-bove, And he leads his chil-dren on To the place where he is gone.

A Cradle Song

Padraic Colum

Waldo Beach, 1985

O men from the fields! Come soft-ly with-in. Tread soft-ly, soft-ly, O men com-ing in. *Ma-vour-neen is go-ing from me and from you, To Ma-ry the Moth-er whose man-tle is blue!

*Irish term for "love."

Text: From *Poems of Padraic Colum*, New York: Macmillan Co., 1932. Reprinted by permission of the Estate of Padraic Colum.
Music: © 1991 Waldo Beach.

From reek of the smoke and cold of the floor, And the

peer - ing of things a - cross the half door. O

men from the fields! Soft, soft - ly come through—

Ma - ry puts round him her man - tle of blue.

O Little Town of Bethlehem

FOREST GREEN   8.6.8.6.7.6.8.6

English folk melody
Adapt. and arr. Ralph Vaughan Williams (1872-1958)

Phillips Brooks, 1868

1. O lit - tle town of Beth-le - hem, How still we see thee lie!
2. For Christ is born of Ma - ry; And gath-ered all a - bove,
3. How si - lent-ly, how si - lent-ly, The won-drous gift is given!
4. O ho - ly Child of Beth-le - hem, De - scend to us, we pray;

A - bove thy deep and dream-less sleep The si - lent stars go by.
While mor-tals sleep, the an - gels keep Their watch of won-dering love.
So God im-parts to hu - man hearts The bless-ings of his heaven.
Cast out our sin and en - ter in, Be born in us to - day.

Yet in thy dark streets shin - eth The ev - er - last - ing light;
O morn-ing stars, to - geth - er Pro - claim the ho - ly birth!
No ear may hear his com - ing, But in this world of sin,
We hear the Christ-mas an - gels The great glad tid - ings tell;

The hopes and fears of all the years Are met in thee to - night.
And prais - es sing to God the King, And peace to all on earth.
Where meek souls will re - ceive him, still The dear Christ en-ters in.
O come to us, a - bide with us, Our Lord Em - man-u - el!

Music: From the *English Hymnal.* Reprinted by permission of Oxford University Press, London.

56

Break Forth, O Beauteous Heavenly Light

ERMUNTRE DICH   8.7.8.7.8.8.7.7

Johann Rist, 1641
Trans. John Troutbeck, 1873

Johann Schop, 1641
Harm. J. S. Bach, 1734

Break forth, O beau-teous heaven-ly light, And ush-er in the morn-ing. You shep-herds, shud-der not with fright, But hear the an-gel's warn-ing. This Child, now weak in in-fan-cy, Our con-fi-dence and joy shall be; The power of Sa-tan break-ing, Our peace e-ter-nal mak-ing.

Chill of the Nightfall

Timothy Dudley-Smith, 1978

Waldo Beach, 1982

difficult

1. Chill of the night - fall, lamps in the win - dows,
2. Si - lence of mid - night, voic - es of an - gels,
3. Splen - dor of star - light high on the hill - side

Let - ting their light fall clear on the snow;
Sing - ing to bid night yield to the dawn;
Faint in the far light burn - ing be - low;

Bit - ter De - cem - ber bids us re - mem - ber
Dark - ness is end - ed, sin - ners be - friend - ed,
Kneel - ing be - fore him shep - herds a - dore him,

Christ in the sta - ble long, long a - go.
Where in the sta - ble Je - sus is born.
Christ in the sta - ble long, long a - go.

Brightly

4. Glo - ry of day - break! Sor - rows and shad - ows,

Sud - den - ly they break forth in - to morn;

Sing out and tell now all shall be well now,

For in the sta - ble Je - sus is born!

See Amid the Winter's Snow

HUMILITY   7.7.7.7 with refrain

Edward Caswall, 1858

John Goss, 1871

1. See a - mid   the win - ter's snow, Born for us   on earth be - low,
2. Say, you ho - ly shep-herds, say, Tell your joy - ful news   to - day.
3. "As we watched at dead of   night, There ap-peared a   won - drous light;

See,   the gen - tle Lamb ap - pears, Prom-ised from e - ter - nal years.
Why   have you now left   your sheep   On   the lone - ly   moun - tain steep?
An - gels sing-ing 'Peace on earth'   Told   us   of the   Sav - ior's birth."

Refrain

Hail that ev - er - bless-ed morn,   Hail re-demp-tion's hap - py   dawn,

Sing through all Je - ru - sa-lem: Christ is born in   Beth-le - hem.

Infant Holy, Infant Lowly

W ŻŁOBIE LEŻY   4.4.7.4.4.7.4.4.4.4.7

Polish carol
Arr. Edith M. G. Reed, 1926
Polish carol
Trans. Edith M. G. Reed, 1925
Harm. Austin C. Lovelace, 1964

1. In - fant ho - ly, in - fant low - ly, For his bed a cat - tle
2. Flocks were sleep - ing, shep-herds keep - ing Vig - il till the morn-ing

stall; Ox - en low - ing, lit - tle know-ing, Christ the babe is Lord of
new Saw the glo - ry, heard the sto - ry, Tid - ings of a gos-pel

all. Swift are wing - ing an - gels sing - ing, No - els ring - ing, tid - ings
true. Thus re - joic - ing, free from sor - row, Prais-es voic - ing, greet the

Interlude, Ending

bring-ing: Christ the babe is Lord of all.
mor-row: Christ the babe was born for you.

Music: Harmonization © 1965 Abingdon Press. Used by permission.

61

Go, Tell It on the Mountain

GO TELL IT   7.6.7.6 with refrain

African-American spiritual
Stanzas, John W. Work II (1872–1925)

African-American spiritual
Arr. John W. Work III, 1940
Harm. and adapt. Melva Wilson Costen, 1987

I Wonder as I Wander

I WONDER AS I WANDER   Irregular

Appalachian carol
John Jacob Niles
Harm. John Ferguson, 1973

Appalachian carol

1. I won-der as I wan-der, out un-der the sky, How
Je - sus the Sav - ior did come for to die For
poor or' - nary peo - ple like you and like I; I
won - der as I wan - der, out un - der the sky.

2. When Ma - ry birthed Je - sus, 'twas in a cow's stall, With
wise men and farm - ers and shep - herds and all. But
high from God's heav - en a star's light did fall, The
prom - ise of a - ges it did then re - call.

3. If Je - sus had want - ed for an - y wee thing, A
star in the sky or a bird on the wing, Or
all of God's an - gels in heaven for to sing, He
sure - ly could have it, 'cause he was the King.

4. I won - der as I wan - der, out un - der the sky, How
Je - sus the Sav - ior did come for to die For
poor or' - nary peo - ple like you and like I; I
won - der as I wan - der, out un - der the sky.

Christmas Prayers

Almighty God, whose blessed Son was born not into a mansion of wealth, to the mighty and the proud, but in a stable, to plain and poor folk, teach us as we celebrate again his birth, that the true riches of life abundant are found in humility of heart, in simplicity, and in faithful service to those whose needs we can meet, so that we may honor the coming of Christ in spirit and in truth. *Amen.*

We rejoice, O God, at the mystery and the miracle of Christmas, at the light shining in our darkness, a light that no dread of war, no pain of human suffering, no cloud of despair can dim or put out. By that light, we pray, lead us from the tangle of our bewildered ways, from the shadows of fear, from the thickets of strife, to set our feet on the clear paths of peace, confidence, and righteousness that lead to your kingdom. *Amen.*

On this holy night of the birth of your Son, as once long ago shepherds tending their flocks heard the choir of angels singing "Glory to God, peace on the earth," may we too hear again in our homes, in our offices, in our fields and factories, the high song of angelic praise. Then let us in spirit come in haste and joy to the manger of Bethlehem to kneel and worship him. *Amen.*

A Christmas Litany of Praise

LEADER: For the magic and the mystery of this season,
which quickens our spirits with anticipation
and brings to remembrance angel voices
and a far star shining in the East,

PEOPLE: We give you thanks and praise, O God.

LEADER: For the gift of your Word made flesh in Christ, to dwell
among us for the redemption of the world,

PEOPLE: We give you thanks and praise, O God.

LEADER: For the warm pleasures of hearth and home,
for candlelight and holly berry, for loving hands
that prepare food and drink, for the eager joy
in children's faces looking up in wonder and delight,

PEOPLE: We give you thanks and praise, O God.

LEADER: For music-making and holy merriment, for legends
told in verse and song, that echo here the angelic choir,
as when the morning stars sang together and
all the people of God shouted for joy,

PEOPLE: We give you thanks and praise, O God.

LEADER: For daily tasks to which we return from the manger
with hearts renewed, to ease the suffering of neighbors
far and near, to nurture the young, to turn the despair
of loved ones into hope, to fill lonely spaces
with friendship, to give of ourselves in the myriad ways
that weave the fabric of community, and keep it strong,
and find the splendor of your glory shining in them all,

PEOPLE: We give you thanks and praise, O God.

Epiphany

EPIPHANY LECTIONARY READINGS

Old Testament
Isaiah 60:1–6

New Testament

Matthew 2:1–12
Mark 1:4–11, or
Matthew 3:13–17, or
Luke 3:15–17, 21–22
John 2:1–11

Christmas

The snow is full of silver light
Spilled from the heavens' tilted cup
And, on this holy, tranquil night,
The eyes of all are lifted up
To see the promise written fair,
The hope of peace for all on earth,
And hear the singing bells declare
The marvel of the dear Christ's birth.
The way from year to year is long
And though the road be dark so far,
Bright is the manger, sweet the song,
The steeple rises to the Star.

Faith Baldwin

The Star

We know not through what trackless space of night,
Nor from what realms it brought the radiant light,
What deserts, seas, or gardens felt its ray,
Before its beams touched where the Christ Child lay.

Men may not sight it, measure its vast swing,
Nor time its balance like a temporal thing;
Yet close, at Christmas, gleams the age-old sign
Of Bethlehem's Star, above your heart and mine.

Ida Norton Munson

Oh, Bring Not Gold!

Oh, bring not gold this Christmas night!
    'Twas gold that Gaspar bore.
And bring not frankincense such as
    Was borne by Melchior:
Nor myrrh whose dusky breath perfumed
    Slim hands of Balthasar!
No! bring not these, the gifts of earth,
    However rich you are!

What has a child to do with gold
    And greedy bartering?
And what to do with frankincense
    And stilted worshipping?
And what has a child to do with myrrh
    And tombs, death-staled and dim?
Nay, have you coffers, crowns, rich robes,
    Bring not these gifts to him!

But come to him, this Christmas night,
    As once the shepherds came,
With empty hands, yet, in their eyes,
    Burned wonder's subtle flame,
And in their minds was quiet faith,
    And in their hearts the tall
White flower of love. Such gifts they bore
    Who bore no gifts at all.

Now, in your eyes, let wonder be;
    Let love be in your heart;
Faith in your mind, unworldly things
    Not sold in any mart—
And yet, a Child has need of these.
    Who bear such gifts, draw nigh!
For these give peace, not frankincense,
    Nor myrrh, nor gold can buy.

Violet Alleyn Storey

Babushka
A Russian Legend

Babushka sits before the fire
Upon a winter's night;
The driving winds heap up the snow,
Her hut is snug and tight;
The howling winds—they only make
Babushka's fire more bright!

She hears a knocking at the door:
So late—who can it be?
She hastes to lift the wooden latch,
No thought of fear has she;
The wind-blown candle in her hand
Shines out on strangers three.

Their beards are white with age, and snow
That in the darkness flies;
Their floating locks are long and white,
But kindly are their eyes
That sparkle underneath their brows,
Like stars in frosty skies.

"Babushka, we have come from far,
We tarry but to say,
A little Prince is born this night,
Who all the world shall sway.
Come join the search; come, go with us,
Who go our gifts to pay."

Babushka shivers at the door;
"I would I might behold
The little Prince who shall be King
But ah! the night is cold,
The wind so fierce, the snow so deep,
And I, good sirs, am old."

The strangers three, no word they speak,
But fade in snowy space!
Babushka sits before her fire,
And dreams, with wistful face:
"I would that I had questioned them,
So I the way might trace!

"When morning comes with blessèd light,
I'll early be awake;
My staff in hand I'll go—perchance,
Those strangers I'll o'ertake;
And, for the Child some little toys
I'll carry, for His sake."

The morning came, and, staff in hand,
She wandered in the snow,
She asked the way of all she met,
But none the way could show.
"It must be farther yet," she sighed;
"Then farther will I go."

And still, 'tis said, on Christmas Eve,
When high the drifts are piled,
With staff, with basket on her arm,
Babushka seeks the Child:
At every door her face is seen—
Her wistful face and mild!

Her gifts at every door she leaves;
She bends and murmurs low,
Above each little face half-hid
By pillows white as snow:
"And is He here?" Then softly sighs,
"Nay, farther must I go."

Edith M. Thomas

The Flight Into Egypt
From "For the Time Being:
A Christmas Oratorio"

Well, so that is that. Now we must dismantle the tree,
Putting the decorations back into their cardboard boxes—
Some have got broken—and carrying them up to the attic.
The holly and the mistletoe must be taken down and burnt,
And the children got ready for school. There are enough
Left-overs to do, warmed-up, for the rest of the week—
Not that we have much appetite, having drunk such a lot,
Stayed up so late, attempted—quite unsuccessfully—
To love all of our relatives, and in general
Grossly overestimated our powers. Once again
As in previous years we have seen the actual Vision and failed
To do more than entertain it as an agreeable
Possibility, once again we have sent Him away,
Begging though to remain His disobedient servant,
The promising child who cannot keep His word for long.
The Christmas Feast is already a fading memory,
And already the mind begins to be vaguely aware
Of an unpleasant whiff of apprehension at the thought
Of Lent and Good Friday which cannot, after all, now
Be very far off. But, for the time being, here we all are,
Back in the moderate Aristotelian city
Of darning and the Eight-Fifteen, where Euclid's geometry
And Newton's mechanics would account for our experience,
And the kitchen table exists because I scrub it.
It seems to have shrunk during the holidays. The streets
Are much narrower than we remembered; we had forgotten
The office was as depressing as this. To those who have seen
The Child, however dimly, however incredulously,
The Time Being is, in a sense, the most trying time of all.
For the innocent children who whispered so excitedly
Outside the locked door where they knew the presents to be
Grew up when it opened. Now, recollecting that moment
We can repress the joy, but the guilt remains conscious;
Remembering the stable where for once in our lives
Everything became a You and nothing was an It.
And craving the sensation but ignoring the cause,

We look round for something, no matter what, to inhibit
Our self-reflection, and the obvious thing for that purpose
Would be some great suffering. So, once we have met the Son,
We are tempted ever after to pray to the Father:
"Lead us into temptation and evil for our sake."
They will come, all right, don't worry; probably in a form
That we do not expect, and certainly with a force
More dreadful than we can imagine. In the meantime
There are bills to be paid, machines to keep in repair,
Irregular verbs to learn, the Time Being to redeem
From insignificance. The happy morning is over,
The night of agony still to come; the time is noon:
When the Spirit must practice his scales of rejoicing
Without even a hostile audience, and the Soul endure
A silence that is neither for nor against her faith
That God's Will will be done, that, in spite of her prayers,
God will cheat no one, not even the world of its triumph.

W. H. Auden

For Another Birth

The miracle is now. The place is here.
　No angel's wings. No throne. No diadem.
Yet in this hour locked and rocked with fear, *uncertainty*
　A birth may mark another Bethlehem.

No kings surround a cradle. Crowds roar by. *thru our drunken streets.*
　The shepherds have been missing since the war. *mass develop?*
Yet darkness splinters//as a wintry sky
　Unfolds and holds—again—a burning star.

This is a time for wonders. The world *cosmos* cries
　For revelation, for another birth.
Dry sticks burst into blossom; dead bones rise;
　And prophets whisper to a desperate earth.

Some child unborn may rescue us, for still
　The wise men come with promise of release:
The myrrh of hope, the gold of men's *our* good will,
　The fresh and precious frankincense of peace. *new breath.*

Tonight
Welcome all saints, all saviors of all time.
　Welcome the thorns on every martyr's brow.
Welcome the cross. Welcome the long, slow climb.
　The place is here. The miracle is now.

allow the touch of one so near,
to surprise you
with new birth.

　　　　　　　　　　　Louis Untermeyer

Tonight the divine (Holy One) is again
... breathing the sacred breath of
new virginal life potential,
... creating the Cosmic (C n) here
pregnant with possibilities
within us + our common-Christic
tribal union.

Brightest and Best of the Stars of the Morning

EPIPHANY HYMN   11.10.11.10

Reginald Heber (1783–1826), alt.

J. F. Thrupp (1827–1867)

1. Bright-est and best of the stars of the morn - ing,
2. Cold on his cra - dle the dew - drops are shin - ing;
3. Say, shall we yield him, in cost - ly de - vo - tion,
4. Vain - ly we of - fer each am - ple ob - la - tion;
5. *Bright-est and best of the stars of the morn - ing,

Dawn on our dark - ness, and lend us thine aid;
Low lies his head with the beasts of the stall;
O - dors of E - dom, and of - ferings di - vine,
Vain - ly with gifts would his fa - vor se - cure;
Dawn on our dark - ness, and lend us thine aid;

Star of the East, the hor - i - zon a - dorn - ing,
An - gels a - dore him in slum - ber re - clin - ing,
Gems of the moun - tain, and pearls of the o - cean,
Rich - er by far is the heart's ad - o - ra - tion;
Star of the East, the hor - i - zon a - dorn - ing,

Guide where our in - fant Re - deem - er is laid.
Mak - er, and Mon - arch, and Sav - ior of all.
Myrrh from the for - est, or gold from the mine?
Dear - er to God are the prayers of the poor.
Guide where our in - fant Re - deem - er is laid.

* Stanza 5 unison.

The Christmas Star

Nancy Byrd Turner

Waldo Beach, 1989

1. High in the heavens a sin-gle star, Of pure im-per-ish-a-ble light;
2. Stars rise and set, that star shines on; Songs fail but still that mus-ic beats

Out on the desert strange and far, Dim rid-ers rid-ing through the night:
Through all the a-ges come and gone, In lane and field and cit-y streets.

A-bove a hill-top sud-den song, Sil-ver trum-pets down the sky—
And we who catch the Christ-mas gleam, Watch with chil-dren on the hill,

And all to wel-come One so young He scarce could lift a cry.
We know, we know it is no dream. He stands a-mong us still.

Text: Used by permission of Nancy Byrd Turner.
Music: © 1991 Waldo Beach.

God of the Starfields

Albert F. Bayly (1901–1984)

Waldo Beach, 1980

1. God of the star - fields, Sown with light's splen - dor,
2. Ser-aphs be - fore him Cried "Ho - ly, ho - ly";
3. But now, be - hold them! Ma - gi come rid - ing.

Thy word a - far wields In - fin - ite sway.
Swift to a - dore him, Serv - ing his will.
Wis - dom has told them Here they will find

Yet in a sta - ble, Born of a vir - gin,
Now in a man - ger Cra - dled with cat - tle,
King of all na - tions, Lord of all crea - tures,

In - fant in man - ger, Thy great-ness lay.
On - ly poor shep - herds Wor-ship him still.
Rul - er and Sav - ior, Help of man - kind.

Text: From Albert F. Bayly, *Again I Say Rejoice: Hymns and Verses,* © copyright 1967 by A. F.
Reprinted by permission of Oxford University Press, London.
Music: © 1991 Waldo Beach.

Songs of Thankfulness and Praise

SALZBURG   7.7.7.7 D

Jacob Hintze, 1678
Harm. J. S. Bach (1685–1750)
As in *Hymns Ancient and Modern,* 1861

Christopher Wordsworth (1807–1885)

1. Songs of thank-ful - ness and praise, Je - sus, Lord, to thee we raise;
2. Man - i - fest at Jor-dan's stream, Proph-et, Priest, and King su-preme;
3. Man - i - fest in mak-ing whole Pal - sied limbs and faint-ing soul;
4. Grant us grace to see thee, Lord, Pres - ent in thy ho - ly Word;

Man - i - fest-ed by the star To the sa - ges from a - far,
And at Ca - na wed-ding guest In thy God-head man - i - fest;
Man - i - fest in val - iant fight, Quell-ing all the dev - il's might;
Grace to im - i - tate thee now And be pure, as pure art thou;

Branch of roy - al Da - vid's stem In thy birth at Beth-le - hem:
Man - i - fest in power di - vine, Chang-ing wa - ter in - to wine;
Man - i - fest in gra - cious will, Ev - er bring-ing good from ill:
That we might be - come like thee At thy great e - piph-a - ny,

An - thems be to thee ad - dressed,
An - thems be to thee ad - dressed,   God in flesh made man - i - fest.
An - thems be to thee ad - dressed,
And may praise thee, ev - er blest,

80

Rise Up, Shepherd, and Follow

African-American spiritual   African-American spiritual

1. There's a star in the East on Christ - mas morn,
2. If you take good heed to the an - gel's words,

Rise up, shep-herd, and fol - low, It will lead to the place where the
Rise up, shep-herd, and fol - low, You'll for - get your flocks, you'll for-

Christ was born, Rise up, shep-herd, and fol - low.
get your herds, Rise up, shep-herd, and fol - low.

Fol - low, fol - low, Rise up, shep-herd, and fol - low,

Fol-low the Star of Beth-le - hem, Rise up, shep-herd, and fol-low.

O Morning Star, How Fair and Bright

WIE SCHÖN LEUCHTET   8.8.7.8.8.7.4.8.4.8

Philipp Nicolai, 1599
Trans. Catherine Winkworth, 1863
Stanza 3 as in *Lutheran Book of Worship*

Philipp Nicolai, 1599
Harm. J. S. Bach, 1740

1. O Morn-ing Star, how fair and bright Thou beam-est forth in truth and light! O Sov-ereign meek and low-ly! Thou root of Jes-se, Da-vid's Son, My Lord and Sav-ior, thou hast won My heart to serve thee sole-ly! Thou art ho-ly,

2. Thou heaven-ly bright-ness! Light di-vine! O deep with-in my heart now shine, And make thee there an al-tar! Fill me with joy and strength to be Thy mem-ber, ev-er joined to thee In love that can-not fal-ter! Toward thee long-ing

3. What joy to know, when life is past, The Lord we love is first and last, The end and the be-gin-ning! He will one day, O glo-rious grace, Trans-port us to that hap-py place Be-yond all tears and sin-ning! A-men! A-men!

Fair and glo-rious, all-vic-to-rious, Rich in bless - ing,
Doth pos-sess me; turn and bless me; Here in sad - ness
Come, Lord Je - sus! Crown of glad-ness, We are yearn - ing

Rule and might o'er all pos - sess - ing.
Eye and heart long for thy glad - ness!
For the day of thy re - turn - ing.

Sing We Now of Christmas

FRENCH CAROL   11.11.10.11

French carol

French carol
Harm. Martin Shaw, 1928

1. Sing we now of Christ-mas, No - el sing we here!
2. An - gels called to shep-herds, "Leave your flocks at rest,
3. In Beth - le - hem they found him; Jo - seph and Ma - ry mild,
4. From the east - ern coun - try Came the kings a - far,
5. Gold and myrrh they took there, Gifts of great-est price;

Hear our grate-ful prais - es To the babe so dear.
Jour - ney forth to Beth - lehem, Find the child so blest."
Seat - ed by the man - ger, Watch-ing the ho - ly Child.
Bear - ing gifts to Beth - lehem, Guid - ed by a star.
There was never a sta - ble So like par - a - dise.

Refrain

Sing we No - el, the King is born, No - el!

Sing we now of Christ - mas, Sing we now No - el!

Music: Harmonization from the *Oxford Book of Carols,* by permission of Oxford University Press.

84

As with Gladness Men of Old

DIX   7.7.7.7.7.7

Conrad Kocher, 1838
Abr. William Henry Monk, 1861
Harm. *The English Hymnal,* 1906

William Chatterton Dix, c. 1858

1. As with glad-ness men of old Did the guid-ing star be-hold;
2. As with joy-ful steps they sped To that low-ly man-ger bed,
3. As they of-fered gifts most rare At that man-ger rude and bare;
4. Ho-ly Je-sus, ev-ery day Keep us in the nar-row way;

As with joy they hailed its light, Lead-ing on - ward, beam-ing bright;
There to bend the knee be-fore Him whom heaven and earth a-dore;
So may we with ho-ly joy, Pure, and free from sin's al-loy,
And, when earth-ly things are past, Bring our ran-somed souls at last

So, most gra-cious Lord, may we Ev - er-more be led to thee.
So may we with will-ing feet Ev - er seek thy mer-cy seat.
All our cost-liest trea-sures bring, Christ, to thee, our heaven-ly King.
Where they need no star to guide, Where no clouds thy glo-ry hide.

When Jesus Went to Jordan's Stream

CHRIST UNSER HERR ZUM JORDAN KAM   8.7.8.7.8.7.8.7.7

Martin Luther, 1541
Para. F. Bland Tucker, 1977

Harm. J. S. Bach (1685–1750)

1. When Je - sus went to Jor - dan's stream His Fa-ther's will o - bey - ing, And was bap-tized by John, there came A voice from heav - en say - ing, "This is my dear be - lov - ed Son, Up - on whom rests my fa - vor." And

2. The Ho - ly Spir - it then was shown, A dove on him de - scend - ing; So Tri - une God is here made known In Christ as love un - end - ing. He taught, he healed, he raised the dead, Yet, in his great en - deav - or To

3. He came by wa - ter and by blood To heal our lost con - di - tion; He cleans - es, rec - on - ciles to God, And gives the Great Com - mis - sion. Then let us not heed world - ly lies Nor rest up - on our mer - it, But

till God's will is ful - ly done He will not bend or
save us, his own blood was shed; But death could hold him
trust in Christ who will bap - tize With wa - ter and the

wa - ver, For he is Christ the Sav - ior.
nev - er. He rose, and lives for - ev - er.
Spir - it That we may life in - her - it.

Epiphany Prayers

Eternal God, by the light of whose star the wise men from the East were led to Bethlehem, show forth anew the radiant star of your Spirit, we pray, that we may be drawn from the far places of our worldly concerns to whatever near manger cradles your blessed Son, bringing him our gifts of tribute and devotion. *Amen.*

O God, whose spirit transcends all empty forms of casual worship, whose living Word is lost in the many easy words of our formal rituals, baptize us afresh in this Epiphany season with the water of the Holy Spirit, as was Christ himself on Jordan's bank, filling the emptiness of our listless worship and enflaming us with the fire of zeal for your kingdom and your righteousness, that we may live out your power and presence in the world. Through Jesus Christ our Lord. *Amen.*

Almighty God, whose Son at the wedding feast in Cana turned the water into wine, now again, by the silent miracles of your grace, turn the tedium of our daily routines into the bright and sparkling wine of your spirit of love, that our lives may be renewed in zest and inspired with joy. Through Jesus Christ our Lord. *Amen.*

A Litany for Epiphany

LEADER: For the splendor of starlight that manifests by night the wonder of the skies, and now shines in our hearts with the memory of his birth, who came as a light to the Gentiles and for the glory of your people Israel,

PEOPLE: We give you thanks and praise, O God.

LEADER: As once the wise men beheld the shining star in the East and were led by its light to bring their gifts to the Christ child in the manger, grant us the wisdom to learn where we may find him in our daily lives, and may be led to bring our gifts of devotion and service.

PEOPLE: This we ask in his name, O Lord.

LEADER: For the descent of your Holy Spirit into our cheerless lives, inspiring us with renewals of confident faith, for our baptism with the refreshing waters of your grace, and for the wonders of your forgiving power that surprise us with joy and turn us from despair and dread into new life and new hope,

PEOPLE: We give you thanks and praise, O God.

Index of Names

Index of Titles and First Lines

Italic type is used for poetry and liturgy.